THE THEATRE
of
CRUELTY

*The Atrocities
Committed Against Catholics
by Protestant Schismatics
in the 16th Century (1578)*

By

Richard Verstegan

Edited and translated by
Fr. Robert Nixon, OSB

SENSUS FIDELIUM
PRESS

Translated by Fr. Robert Nixon, OSB

ISBN: 978-1-962639-68-2

Book Cover, Book Interior, and E-book Design by Amit Dey (amitdey2528@gmail.com)
For more information, please visit sensusfideliumpress.com

Table of Contents

Translator's Introduction

The atrocities and crimes committed by the schismatics and heretics of 16th Century tend to be glossed over in most widely read histories. One the one hand, followers of Protestantism are not keen to recognize these acts of violence themselves; and Catholics, perhaps in a misguided spirit of generosity and tolerance, generally do not dwell upon them. Moreover, it must be admitted that they scarcely make for pleasant reading.

Nevertheless, the atrocities and persecutions endured by Catholics during the time of the so-called 'Reformation' are justifiably comparable with those suffered by the Jews during the Nazi era. They are certainly no less diabolical, cruel and evil—indeed, perhaps even more so, as the following pages will reveal.

The following book is essential a translation (or, in some instances, adaptation) of a work entitled *Theatrum Crudelitatum Haereticorum Nostri Temporis* [*Theatre of the Cruelties of the Heretics of our Times*]. This significant and unique book, first published in Antwerp in 1578 by an Englishman, variously known as Richard Rowlands and Richard Verstegan, describes the varied and horrendous acts of torture and depravity committed by Protestant schismatics against Catholics during his own times. Richard Verstegan (1550-1640) was born in London, of a Dutch father and English mother. He converted to Catholicism at a young age, and remained a devout and life-long supporter of the one true Church. In particular, he was very active as an underground publisher and purveyor of books, including Catholic devotional and theological works, which were then illegal in England and many other parts of Europe. His own *Theatrum Crudelitatum* was very widely circulated and went through many editions and printings—a remarkable achievement, given the strict control of information and literature which Protestant regimes imposed.

The present translation presents the essential components of the *Theatrum Crudelitatum,* which include both illustrations and descriptions. In some cases, these have been supplemented and augmented with material from other contemporary historical sources. These other sources include the *Commentarius breuis rerum in orbe gestarum ab anno 1500 usque ad annum 1566* of Laurentius Surius (1567), *De Signis Ecclesiae Dei* of Tommaso Bozio (1591), and the *Speculum Haereticae Crudelitatis* of Arnold Havens (1609). The substantial agreement of these various sources is compelling evidence of their veracity.

In certain instances, some liberty has been taken in the wording and formatting of the work, to improve it clarity for the contemporary reader. A number of extremely shocking incidents have been judiciously modified in translation, to make the book suitable for persons of all ages. Nevertheless, it remains a frightening and, in some instances, harrowing work.

It is the hope of the translator that this work will not of interest not only to the scholar and historian, but may awaken awareness of the demonic evil which often lurks behind the mask of so-called 'Reform.'

Fr. Robert Nixon,
Monastery of the Most Holy Trinity,
New Norcia, Western Australia

Author's Preface:
The Origin, Continuity and Success of the Catholic Faith, and the Evil Effects of Heresy in Recent Times

The Catholic, apostolic and Roman Church, from the time of the Ascension of Christ our Savior into Heaven, has continued inviolate for almost 1,500 years, supported by the uninterrupted and legitimate authority of the successors of St. Peter. During this time, it has constantly retained and preserved the purity and integrity of faith and religion.

At various times throughout history, however, many and varied types of heretics had emerged, who were recognized as perfidious deserters of the true Church. These attempted to persecute and fight against the Catholic Church, but were continually refuted and confounded. And so, in due course, they became extinct, together with all the authorities who had supported them.

But in our own age, Martin Luther, who treacherously deserted the holy Catholic Church, has formulated new heresies, whose wickedness and madness were unheard of in former terms. Out of this as their source of origin, innumerable sects of depraved opinions have now emerged, both those who hold to Luther's views and those who dissent from him. Among the latter group, the Calvinists are by far the most detestable.

In our times, these heretics have cast innumerable souls into the depth of hell. Furthermore, they have slaughtered countless human beings, caused sedition and division within Christian nations, and spread devastation over the virtually the entire globe of the earth.

In this volume, the cruelties and atrocities which always accompany and spring from these heresies will be illustrated and described. In this way, their true and diabolic nature will be exposed and proven to the reader.

I. The Cruelty and Inhumanity of the Schismatics of England under the Reign of King Henry VII

I n this current rebellion against the Son of God and His holy Catholic Church, which was instigated by Martin Luther, an apostate Augustinian monk, in Saxony and Germany, virtually all of Germany was first infected with violence. Then John Calvin, leading a sect of vile heretics in Switzerland, have poured out innocent blood with all cruelty and inhumanity. From these dreadful atrocities, it is easy to determine how bitter and black is the hatred which these heretics bear towards Our Lord Jesus Christ and His holy Church. This is clear when one considers both the barbarity and inhumanity of the deeds of these servants of Satan, as well as the fruits of their work—namely the overturning and despoiling of innumerable monasteries, churches, chapels and sacred places. These were all places originally raised up and used by our Christian forefathers for calling upon God and offering to Him the sacrifice of our salvation, and performing other acts of devotion.

Henry VIII, the King of England, despite not being an adherent to the doctrines of either Luther or Calvin, nevertheless has likewise abandoned the Catholic Church. He was incited not by doctrine, but simply by bold and untamable lust, malice and vice. As if in mad fury, he tore down about 10,000 monasteries, churches and chapels within barely the space of a year. More than 100,000 religious persons were dispossessed and removed from the religious orders to which they were professed, either compelled by force or fear, or tempted with worldly allurements.

Whoever refuses to express public support for the absurd and impious claim of the English monarch to be Head of the Church is subjected to the most dreadful cruelty, far exceeding that of the barbarians or pagans. And these victims include not only commoners, but the most illustrious nobles and most holy bishops and religious. The learned and reverend John Fisher, the Bishop of Rochester, experienced this cruelty, as did the respected and honorable Chancellor of the Kingdom, Sir Thomas More. Both of these were decapitated without mercy, their blood shed as testimony to their love for the Lord Jesus Christ and as evidence of their own unshakable fidelity to his one true Church.

The great theologian Richard Reynolds, a monk of the Order of St. Bridgit of Syon Abbey in London, also fell prey to the vicious persecutions of the English schismatics. Because of his firm and loyal adherence to the true Catholic faith he was subjected to the most gruesome form of death imaginable. After being incarcerated in the dreaded darkness of the Tower of London, he, along with several companions, were dragged through the streets of the city tied to horses until they arrived at their destined place of execution. Then they were suspended from gallows, and while suspended—and still alive—the executioners tore their sides open with a dagger. Their hearts and innards were then removed and cast into fire.

Once their heads had been cut off, the limbs of the bodies of each of these martyrs were affixed to four horses. These horses were then whipped and goaded, compelling them to gallop away in different directions, and thus ripping each of the bodies into four portions. Their mortal remains were then placed in conspicuous public places around the city.

What kind of insane and rabid cruelty is behind such revolting and shameless acts? Truly, this is the iniquity which falsely claims to be based on the Gospel, and yet which casts away all traces of decency, honor and humanity, and surpasses even the ancient tyrants of the pagan people in ruthlessness and impiety!

When King Henry VIII had entered into one of his several unlawful and invalid marriages, he eagerly sought to gain the approval for this union from the Carthusians in England, hoping by this means to demonstrate that his actions were undertaken with the authority and sanction of the Roman Catholic Church. However, the Carthusians naturally refused to give him any token of such approval. In his mad fury, the arrogant king sentenced them all to death. But before accepting the crown of martyrdom, they underwent numerous tortures at the command of the monarch and were thrown into a miserable dungeon and bound down by heavy chains. There, they were subject to further interrogation and inhuman tortures. When all of these measures failed to break their noble resolve and unwavering faith, it was finally decided that they should be executed.

Gallows were made in the form of crosses, and these brave monks were hung from them. Eventually, the ropes by which they were affixed were cut and they fell to the ground, already half dead. Dragged to a blazing bonfire, their innards ripped asunder. Their hearts, still beating, were then seized and cast into the fire. Then their heads were severed, and their bodies torn into four parts. Following this, their remains were displayed in public places, as a gruesome spectacle to all—an object both of horror and of scorn.

Do we need to provide further examples of the cruelty of such heretics? For there were countless others who met their death in ways similar to those described in relation to these Carthusian martyrs—namely of being "hanged, drawn and quartered." Amongst these was Edmund Campion, a faithful and learned Jesuit priest, as well as innumerable other Catholic clergy and religious.

Illustration I

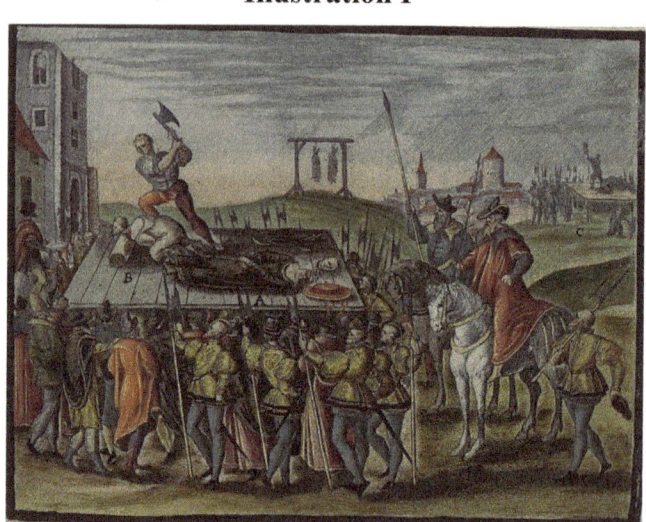

The following events are depicted in Illustration I:

A (slightly below and to the left of the middle): The beheading of St. John Fisher.

B (middle left side of illustration): The beheading of Sir Thomas More, formerly Chancellor of England.

C (upper right of illustration): The beheading of the Blessed Margaret Pole, Countess of Salisbury, and mother of Cardinal Reginald Pole, Archbishop of Canterbury.

Illustration II

The following events are depicted in Illustration II:

A (slightly below and to the left of the middle): Carthusian monks who refused to sanction Henry VIII's divorce were dragged to a place of execution.

B (middle right side of illustration): The same Carthusian monks were hanged from the gallows.

C (lower right of illustration): The same Carthusian monks, having been removed from the gallows still alive, were cut open. Their innards were then cast into a fire, while they looked on. Finally, they were decapitated, and their bodies torn into four parts by horses impelled to run in different directions.[1]

---

[1] See upper left of illustration.

Illustration III

The following events are depicted in Illustration III:

A (slightly to the right and slightly above the middle of the illustration): Friar John Forest, a Franciscan, was hanged not far from the city of London.

B (in the lower part of the illustration and slightly to the right): A sacred image of King David, the prophet and psalmist, was burnt beneath Friar John, who had attempted to defend it against the iconoclasm of the heretics.

C (middle left of illustration): Many abbots and leaders of convents, worthy of reverence and respect, were strangled, eviscerated, and drawn and quartered.

D (upper right of the illustration): Many bishops suffered the same fate, for no other crime than their loyalty to the Catholic Church.

II. The Horrible Cruelties Committed against Catholics in France, by those who are called Huguenots

The persecutions, slaughters and devastations which occurred in France against the Catholics, and especially against religious and priests, were so great and so appalling that they shall scarcely be able to be believed by future generations. Altars were destroyed, sacred images desecrated, and many churches incinerated. The number of sacred places that were overturned and devastated is almost incredible—something more than ten thousand. And some of these churches and religious houses were converted into stables for horses or used as dens for bandits. More than six hundred monasteries were razed to the ground, and many more were put to flames.

Sacred vessels of gold and silver were plundered, and the proceeds from this wholesale theft were used to finance wars between various provincial rulers. In some cases, it was simply taken by private individuals to enrich their own personal coffers. The Blessed Sacrament itself was often cast to swine, and holy oils were used for cooking.

These vicious heretics buried many of the faithful in the earth, still alive. Infants were cut to pieces and small boys were sliced in half. Unborn infants were ripped from the wombs of pregnant mothers and dashed against rocks—in this way passing over to death before they had yet truly experienced earthly life.

From the turmoil in France instigated by the Protestants, some six thousand priests were subjected to various forms of cruelty and torture before being put to death. An equal number of monks and consecrated men and women of all religious orders also suffered the same fate.

There were, for example, a group of priests who were flayed alive, their skin forcibly removed from their bodies. In this horrendous condition, they were kept alive by their persecutors, until reduced to a state of delirium and frenzy. It was only after some eight or nine days had elapsed that, at last and mercifully, their spirits departed from their skinless bodies.

There were many who were beheaded; many were tortured by being stretched on racks of brass; many who were scorched with flames; and many whose throats were transfixed with iron nails and so, rendered incapable of swallowing, eventually starved to death.

Not a few were suspended from crosses in churches, and many were coated with lard and pulverized brimstone and then cast into fires. Still others were ripped open, and their living entrails torn out and fed to pigs.

Of the vast multitudes who underwent tortures, there were, of course, many who survived, and still a considerable number who survive to this very day. Most of these bear scars and deformities as visible evidence of the atrocities they underwent; either in the form of split nostrils, amputated ears, missing feet which were either hacked or burnt off, and extracted fingernails and toenails. There survive also many who were blinded, crippled or despoiled of their senses through tortures. All of these carry in their bodies visible remnants of the diabolical and inhuman crimes perpetrated by the opponents of the Church and the enemies of the Gospel.

In the township of Longjumeau there was a pious and holy priest who refused to be swayed from his loyalty to the Catholic Church. He was seized by the forces of the schismatics, and his membrum virile was firmly bound with a rope. The other end of this rope was then attached to a horse, and he was dragged for the distance of some three miles. Their victim was then suspended over a scorching fire until he was overcome with smoke and suffocated. Following this, his mortal remains were callously carved up in the manner of a roasted pig.

And in the town of Mont Bruno, the heretics captured a certain Catholic noblewoman, Lady Marendati. They ripped out all the hair from her head, and then scorched the soles of her delicate feet by forcing her to stand, barefoot, on red hot sheets of metal. Next, the edges of the burning metal were applied to her shins, removing pieces of her skin like leather strips. And what happened next cannot be described in writing. It appalls the soul to think about the abysmal depths of depravity and foulness which these wicked and bestial monsters, possessed by the spirit of Satan, inflicted upon this Catholic lady!

In Angoulême, some thirty-two Catholics were taken prisoner, and subjected to three different, and particularly cruel, forms of torture. Some of them were bound together in pairs. The heretics then placed the two captives in close confinement together without any form of food or sustenance. It was the maleficent and revolting intention of their tormentors that eventually hunger would compel the prisoners to turn upon each other as the only available source of food, in acts of foul cannibalism! Others were affixed to ropes, so that their bodies should be very gradually stretched to breaking point over the space of several days. Yet others were tied naked to wooden stakes, with burning torches very slowly applied to their backs—so that their death was onc of drawn-out agony.

Not far from Angoulême, in the parish of Chassenon, there was a Catholic priest called Fr. Louis Fayard. The Calvinist schismatics seized this man, and forcibly placed his hands into a cauldron filled with boiling oil. They compelled him to remain thus, until the flesh was completely cooked and fell clean away from his bones. They then poured the boiling oil down his throat, and finally shot him dead with muskets.

There was one Jean Bacchelon, whom the Calvinists hanged, after flaying the skin from his feet with red hot steel.

Another man, a devout priest called Fr. Octavian Ronitius, they shod with iron horseshoes. These they nailed to his feet, in the same manner in which they are customarily attached to the hoofs of horses. After this, he was bound to a tree and his body was blasted to bloody fragments with lead shot from the schismatic's firearms.

In a village known as Floran, there was a priest who was beaten with rods for so long that he finally died from loss of blood.

In the township of Saint-Macaire in Gascony, the schismatics seized upon the local priest and, while he was still alive, cut open his abdomen and tied his intestines in knots! In the same place, a great many were buried alive, and children were hacked to pieces with swords.

Another priest was also cut open and, still alive, his intestines were stuffed with oats and barley. Then, while the priest lay supine and tied down in this condition, hungry horses were loosened on him. These beasts set upon his stuffed innards greedily, turning him into a kind of human feeding trough.

Churches and monasteries were raided everywhere, falling prey to the insatiable wickedness and thieving avarice of the godless and heretical mobs. And women were not spared from this despoilment—neither consecrated virgins, on account of their modesty and meekness; nor even old ladies, on account of their venerable age. Numberless nuns and religious sisters were violated and raped by these wretches. Many were stripped naked, and then driven out of the convents into full public view. Thus, the shameless gaze of lustful men fell upon these poor and innocent virgins, robbed of all protection and defense.

Illustration IV

The following events are depicted in Illustration IV:

A (left side): The city of Angoulême was besieged by Huguenots, who pledged the safety and religious freedom of its inhabitants if they should open the city to them. However, once the Huguenots had taken control, they proceeded to plunder the township and to torture its Catholic citizens. This included raiding a Franciscan friary. The next day, the venerable superior of that friary, Fr. Michel Grellet, was savagely hanged from a tree. As he was thus murdered, the bestial crowd of heretics who killed him cried out with truly demonic hypocrisy, "Long live the Gospel!"

B (central foreground of the illustration): Friar Jean Viroleau, a lector of the same friary, was similarly inhumanely slaughtered, after first being castrated with a sword.

C (right midground): Fr. Jean Avril, a man in his eighties, had his head split upon with a double-edged sword. After this, his corpse was hurled into a latrine.

D (upper right, in the background): Fr. Pierre Bonneau, a Doctor of Theology, was detained in a miserable dungeon continuously for some eight months. After this, he was hanged to death from a tree outside the city walls.

Illustration V

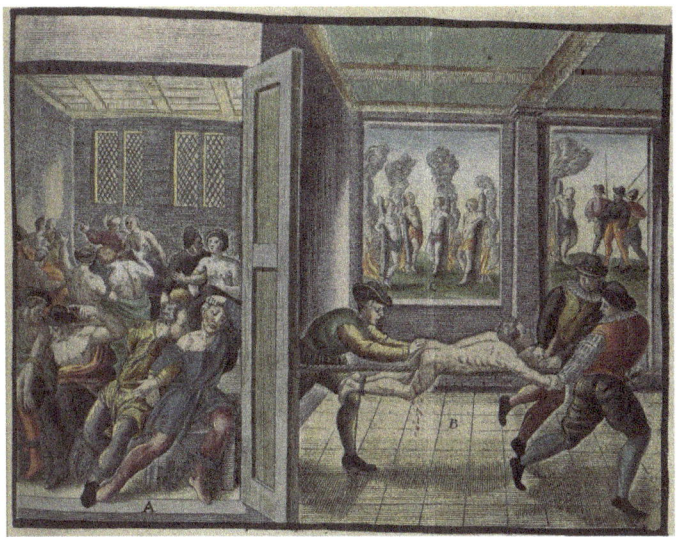

The following events are depicted in Illustration V:

A (left side of the illustration): In a township called Papin, within the municipality of the city of Angoulême, some thirty-two Catholics were taken as prisoners by the heretics. These were put to death by three different methods. Some (A) were confined within a chamber and chained together in pairs. Then they were deprived of all food and water. It was the depraved hope of their captors that they would eventually be compelled to commit acts of cannibalism. This, of course, did not happen; but eventually they perished through starvation.

B (right side of the illustration, in the foreground): Others were painfully stretched out on ropes for a long period of time—several days, in fact—until their bodies were split asunder.

C (right side of the illustration, in the background): Other prisoners were tied to poles, and held a little above the ground. Fires where then applied to the backs, causing them to cook to death in a slow and agonizing fashion.

Illustration VI

The following events are depicted in Illustration VI:

A (right side of the illustration): The leaders of the Huguenots, who seized a particular town called Mont Bruno, often visited a certain noblewomen called Lady Marendati, She treated them with all kindness and civility. But, after accepting her hospitality, the set upon her viciously. They applied burning sheets of metal, made red-hot in a fire, to the soles of her feet, and tortured her in other ways which are too grotesque to be described in writing. After that, they raided her house of its riches.

B (left side of the illustration, in the foreground): Master Jean Arnold, Vicar-General of the King of France, was appointed as a magistrate in the city of Angoulême. After it was seized by the heretics, he was captured. His limbs were cruelly mutilated, and then he was strangled to death in his own home.

C (right side of the illustration, in the background): A certain Catholic widow in her sixties was captured in the same city. She was painfully dragged by her hair by the Huguenot villains through the squares and streets of the town.

Illustration VII

The following events are depicted in Illustration VII:

A (lower right foreground): Not far from Angoulême, in the parish of Chassenon, there was a Catholic priest called Fr. Louis Fayard. The Calvinist schismatics seized this man, and forcibly placed his hands into a cauldron filled with boiling oil, until the flesh came off the bone.

B (left side of the illustration, in the foreground): The Huguenots captured a faithful priest, Fr. Colin Guillebaut, and enclosed him, still alive, in a kind of perforated wooden casket. They then poured boiling oil through the holes in the casket, inflicting unbelievable torments on him until he finally expired.

C (center of illustration, midground): In the parish popularly known as Rivieres, a certain faithful Catholic man was viciously attacked by the heretics. While he was still alive, they pulled out his tongue until it reached beyond his chin—and then they viciously hacked it off.

Illustration VIII

The following events are depicted in Illustration VIII:

A (lower left, foreground): A certain faithful priest, Fr. Octavian Ronitius, fell into the hands of the demonic schismatics. The applied horseshoes to the soles of his feet with nails, in the way that horses are shod. After this, he was tied to a tree and blasted with lead shot from the firearms of his captors.

B (left side of the illustration, in the midground): Fr. Francois Raboteau, a parish priest, was similarly captured and tied to an ox drawing a plough. Such violent whipping and goading were then applied to the beast that the poor priest was eventually dashed to death.

C (left of illustration, in the background): A vast number of other Catholics were killed by the Calvinists in similar ways. One of them, Nicolas Guiveus, a fabric merchant, was bound to a tree, and then perforated with javelins until he expired. As he suffered and died, he never ceased to call upon the holy name of Jesus Christ. In the parish of Angoulême alone, within barely the space of two years, over one hundred and twenty faithful Catholics were cruelly killed, including persons of both sexes, priests and laity, nobility and commoners alike.

Illustration IX

The following events are depicted in Illustration IX:

A (lower right, foreground): In the town of Houdan, in the diocese of Chartres, the heretics captured a certain priest and compelled him to offer the sacrifice of the Mass. They did this for no other reason than to mock him and desecrate the Sacrament. While he said the Mass, they continually slapped and punched him in the face. Nevertheless, this brave priest, who was to become a martyr, persevered with the holy Mass, despite being covered in his own flowing blood. After he had completed the consecration, the heretics then seized the precious Body and Blood of Christ, and threw it to the ground, trampling it underfoot.

B (upper left): They heretics then tied to same priest to the crucifix in the church. There, they proceeded to blast him with their muskets, thus sending him to his death.

C (center left of illustration): In a village called Floran, a faithful priest was captured. He was then stripped and scourged with rods, until he bled to death. His murderer is said to have boasted that it was the seventeenth such priest he had killed in this manner.

Illustration X

The following events are depicted in Illustration X:

A (left side of illustration): In the city of Cléry, after the cathedral had been raided of its treasures, the Huguenots sacrilegiously desecrated the tomb of Louis XI, King of France. After extracting his mortal remains, they proceeded to incinerate his skeleton in the city streets, in order to annihilate all memory of this Catholic monarch.

B (upper center): In a village called Pat, which is about six or seven miles from the city of Orleans, twenty-five faithful Catholics were violently set upon by a rabid mob of heretics. Filled with terror, they sought refuge in the belltower of the local church. But their merciless attackers set this alight. Eventually, compelled by the flames and smoke, the victims had no choice but to throw themselves from the tall tower. There, the heretical killers awaited them, like ravenous beasts of prey, to slaughter them.

C (center right, midground: Innumerable priests were also captured, bound to the tails of horses, and then led off to their death.

Illustration XI

The following events are depicted in Illustration XI:

A (lower right side of illustration): In the township of Saint-Macaire in Gascony, the schismatics seized upon the local priest and, while he was still alive, cut open his abdomen and tied his intestines in knots, winding them around a wooden staff while he looked on.

B (center of illustration): Many of the Catholic clergy who were captured by the heretics were buried alive.

C (upper left, background): The Huguenots did not spare even the infants of Catholic mothers, many of whom they put to death at the edge of the sword without mercy.

D (lower left, foreground): In the district of Manciet, a certain very elderly priest was captured. The heretics cut off a part of his body, roasted it upon the fire while he looked on, then forced him to consume it! Not content with this, they then cut him open (while he was still alive), to examine the content of his innards.

Illustration XII

The following events are depicted in Illustration XII:

A (foreground, slightly to the right of the center): Such was the diabolic arrogance and vanity of the Huguenots that one of them made for himself a necklace out of the amputated ears of his victims. This he wore around proudly, as if it were an item of fashion!

B (right foreground): Innumerable priests and religious suffered amputations of their noses and ears and had their eyes gouged out at the hands of the wicked heretics.

C (left foreground): A certain priest was cut open by the heretics and, still alive, his intestines were stuffed with oats and barley. Then, while the poor priest lay on his back in agony, a hungry horse was set upon him, thus turning him into a kind of human feeding trough.

D (upper left): Heretics in the city of Nîmes, in the province of Languedoc, assaulted and beat a great number of the local Catholic faithful. And having beaten them half to death, they then dumped them, still alive, into a deep well to drown.

III. The Brutal Martyrdom of Franciscans Friars at Gorkum in Belgium

Since 1566, there have been various tumults and upheavals within the formerly peaceful lowland provinces of Holland. These testify to the woeful and deplorable extent to which the violence and insanity of the heretics has infected these regions in recent times. There have been numerous outbreaks of bloody slaughter, and churches and monasteries now lie in desolate and pitiful ruins in many places.

A multitude of churches and shrines have been profaned and despoiled of their ornamentation and artwork by the greedy and grasping hands of the ungodly. And the most shocking crimes have been committed against women who have dedicated themselves to a life of chastity for God, with countless nuns and religious sisters being ruthlessly raped by these Calvinist monsters. Moreover, priests and monks have not been spared from the murderous onslaught and hateful fury of the schismatics.

In the Year of Our Lord 1572 against the Franciscan friars in the Dutch town of Gorkum and several others who were with them, including secular priests and members of other religious institutes. These were all seized by desperate and damnable men, and brought before William II de la Marck, the Count of Lummen. This villainous heretic burned with a veritable lust to shed innocent blood and was inflated with both demonic pride and barbaric cruelty. It is reliably reported that he quite literally washed his hands in the blood of slaughtered priests. His cruelty became so notorious through Holland that it was a source of astonishment and scandal and was so extreme that even the Turks themselves were stunned with horror upon hearing of his practices and crimes.

The wickedness began when the Calvinist forces arrested Nicolas Pieck, the superior of the community of Franciscans at Gorkum and a very devout man, along with ten other friars and some diocesan priests. They were held in custody in appalling conditions in a confined and filthy prison. How much evil and maltreatment these men suffered while incarcerated is almost beyond description! And the days and nights they spent languishing in their dungeon cell seemed to drag on interminably.

They were all exposed to insults, mockeries and beatings, and bore brutal and savage mistreatment from the impious soldiers. Indeed, these repulsive ministers of Satan became inebriated virtually everyday and would abuse their prisoners as a kind of drunken sport. They would pound their miserable victims with their fists and kick them with booted feet, pushing and pulling them back and forth, and treating them in other violent ways as the whim took them. And while doing this, they would utter the vilest curses and spiteful maledictions. Indeed, there was no kind of slander or insult which was too depraved for these wretched heretics to pour out upon their helpless captives!

What compelled these soldiers to do this was undoubtedly their own evil and vicious natures, as well as the burning and bitter hatred for all the servants of God which invariably flares up in people of this type.

On a certain night—the first one on which the Franciscans and their associates were imprisoned—after the soldiers had devoured a heavy dinner and glutted themselves with intoxicating liquors, they rushed into the cell where the prisoners were held, with loud, aggressive shouts and rowdy and ugly tumult. They exclaimed to the friars that they would cut off their masculine members, their noses and their ears, and then affix each of them to crosses! It was the custom of these Calvinist schismatics to refer to Catholic priests scornfully as "idolators" and "confectioners of God," and they hurled these blasphemous insults at them freely.

They also dragged in a small set of gallows, hoping to inspire the fear of imminent death into the hearts of their prisoners, although they did not actually hang any of them on that occasion. Rather, they contented themselves with stripping the men naked and binding them, then beating them violently with rods.

Along with the Franciscans, there were also two parish priests from Gorkum. These the guards attempted to extort, in order to obtain from them the wealth of the parishes which they administered. They picked on the younger one in particular, and put a musket to his head, loaded with shot and gunpowder. They demanded not only that he give to them the items of gold and silver owned by his Church, but that he should betray the much more precious treasure of the Blessed Sacrament and his Catholic faith. But fortified by the power of God, the young priest spoke up boldly, asserting the truth of the real presence in the holy Eucharist and declaring himself ready to die before abandoning his faith.

The soldiers were infuriated and frustrated by the noble courage displayed by the pious youth. Seizing the rope cincture from one of the friars, they tied one end of it around his neck and ran it over the top of the door of the prison cell. By pulling and releasing this rope, they were able to lift the unfortunate young priest off the ground and then drop him down again. This they did repeatedly, thus little by little bringing him to the point of asphyxiation. But when they saw that they could not coerce him even by this gruesome means to betray to them the wealth of his parish or to renounce his faith, they gave up. And he slumped to the ground, more dead than alive.

*   *   *

Frustrated by their failure to overcome the fidelity of this young parish priest, the wicked guards next turn their attention to the friars themselves. Firstly, they seized Nicolas Pieck, the superior of the community, grabbing him not as a human being but rather as a beast, or even like some foul assassin or despicable criminal. They set upon him aggressively with virulent verbal abuse and forceful blows, pounding his whole body with fists and clubs.

After this, they took his cincture and fashioned a noose with one end, which was placed around his neck. As with their previous victim, the rope was then stretched over the top of the door of the prison cell. By means of pulling and releasing the rope, Nicolas was repeatedly raised and lowered from the ground, but in a more rapid and violent fashion than they had done before. Every time he was pulled off the ground, the rope would tighten around his throat and bring him close to death. Yet when it was released, such a death—which by that stage he longed for, both as a merciful release and for the glory of martyrdom for the Church of God—would be cruelly drawn away from him. This continued for a prolonged period, until the rope snapped. At this point he slumped to the ground with his head bowed down, displaying no signs of vitality.

The soldiers then approached him to ascertain whether he was really dead or not. They lifted him up to a standing position and then (either to test whether he had any life remaining in him, or as a kind of perverse sport) they applied burning candles to his face, forehead, mouth, cheeks, ears, chin and nose. As this last appendage was scorched, the acrid smoke entered his nostrils and filled his entire skull. But this was not enough for these fiends. For they forced his mouth open and inserted the blazing candle, burning his tongue and the palate of his mouth.

Throughout all of these things, Nicolas did not show any signs of life whatsoever. So the guards threw him to the ground contemptuously, kicking his body, and counting him as one amongst the dead. "Here is the holy monk!" they exclaimed mockingly. "Who wants him?"

Such were the atrocities committed by those schismatic minions of darkness upon that dreadful night. When dawn arose, they returned to the prison cell, expecting to find the dead body of Nicholas (as they thought) still lying where they had left it. Their plan was to cut his corpse into pieces, and then to place portions of it in conspicuous, high places around the city as a public spectacle.

But when they entered the cell, they found their victim of the previous night living and breathing! Filled with unspeakable fury, they began to torment him once more with renewed malice and hatred. They laid into him with their boots, landing swift kicks onto his sides and abdomen. All the while they shouted in rage, "Do you still live, you wretched monk, do you still live?!"

The abuses they committed next are so foul and heinous that it is said that when the prison surgeon eventually saw Nicolas he immediately burst into tears of pity and horror. For the brutal schismatics took a blazing torch and applied it fully to the friar's face, until it was utterly blackened. His neck also was swollen and bloodied, with most of the skin torn off by the friction of the noose around it on the previous night. But in the midst of all this, the holy Franciscan was filled with noble serenity and patience. With an angelic smile, he said, "Oh, how I long to be tortured and torn limb from limb for the sake of my Catholic faith!"

O my Reader, hear now of another most depraved and shocking deed of cruelty! On another night, when the drunken soldiers rushed into the prison cell of the Franciscans to mock and beat them yet again, the leader of their cohort—maddened with alcohol—demanded of the friars, "I want you each to present me your cheeks in turn!"

So they were all compelled to stand in a row. Beginning with the first, the intoxicated commander of the guards slapped each of them on the face. Such was the force and fury of his blows that many lost teeth or had blood spurting out of their nostrils and even eyes. The next day the morning light revealed the disfigured faces of the victims of this abuse, and their cheeks were grotesquely inflated with swelling, just like men who are blowing trumpets.

Abuses and torments similar to these were committed virtually every day. They took place especially at night, after the guards had eaten dinner and partaken heavily in liquor, as was their invariable custom. They would view such acts of bullying and brutality as an amusing joke or amusement for themselves.

And if anyone ever came to visit the captives, the guards would make a point of letting the visitors see and know how much the prisoners were suffering at their hands.

It happened once that a certain French Calvinist soldier was travelling through Holland, and he happened to come to Gorkum. Hearing about the friars who were being held captive in prison, he arranged to be taken to their cell in order to mock and insult them. Now one of the friars happened to be French as well, and when he recognized the soldier as one of his own countrymen, he greeted him in civil fashion in the French language, declaring himself to be a fellow citizen of France. But the soldier—at heart more a barbarian than a Frenchman—pulled out his dagger and threatened to cut off the poor friar's private parts! And, mockingly, he said, "Since you are my countryman, it is I who should be given the fun of hanging you!" And with some savage thrusts of his dagger, he slashed the prisoner's face.

Another example of the heartless cruelty of the heretics, no less wicked than that just described, shall also be related here. For these Calvinist guards, all men of the crudest and most offensive brutality, were once kneeling before their prisoners, in mocking and irreverent imitation of Catholics making confession of their sins. They would then spring up and, uttering insults, rain down slaps and blows upon the friars and priests. It should be noted that in all of this they showed not the slightest mercy towards the advanced age of some of their captives.

Now, one of the priests, who was an elderly man, accepted each of their blows with the most patient endurance. And each time he was struck, he would calmly say, "Thanks be to God!" For this holy man firmly believed in his heart that it was a great privilege to suffer thus for Jesus and for the Catholic religion.

When another of the guards knelt before him and made a mocking and sacrilegious confession of his sins, he asked the priest how he would respond to that. The priest remained serene and undisturbed, and said—with perfect sincerity—"My son, I shall pray to the Lord for you." At this sign of true patience, compassion and charity, the guard exploded in furious rage. "Oh! You shall pray for me, shall you?!" he exclaimed with bitter sarcasm, and set upon his elderly prisoner like a rabid beast. He beat him with such mad fury and savagery that the poor man was left almost dead.

Indeed, it is not surprising that the sincere prayer and display of genuine Christian charity should have infuriated these men, for such things always inflame the utmost fear and hatred in those who are given to the service of evil.

It would be excessively lengthy to describe here each of the instances of mockery, calumny, torture and beating which these holy Franciscans and their associates suffered whilst held in prison at Gorkum. But the few examples given already suffice to demonstrate the wickedness and cruelty of their schismatic persecutors. These godless heretics were in every respect more cruel than the bloodthirsty Scythians and more violent than the barbarian hordes of times of yore. This same insatiable cruelty would eventually bring these faithful Catholics to the grim darkness of death, yet in doing so would reward them with the glorious and eternal crown of holy martyrdom.

*   *   *

These Franciscans and their associates, after having suffered so many dreadful atrocities whilst being held in prison at Gorkum, were eventually placed on a ship to be transported to the city of Brielle. During this voyage they underwent further hardships, including cold (for they had been robbed of virtually all their garments), hunger and mockery. Their experiences while on the ship I shall not describe, lest my narrative become excessively prolix.

Once they had disembarked at Brielle, William de la Marck, the wicked Count of Lummen, came forth to meet them. Inflamed with his characteristic and inveterate hatred towards religious persons, he greeted them with curses, derision, insults and blasphemies, of a virulence that can scarcely be imagined. The prisoners were then taken to where a set of gallows had been erected. Their persecutors, hoping to inspire them with terror, then forced them to process around it. In mockery, they demanded that they kneel before it, and sing the antiphon to the Blessed Virgin, the *Salve Regina*.

Next the band of friars and priests were made to march through the streets of the town. Again, they were compelled to sing, this time the psalms of the Divine Office. The Calvinist guards exclaimed in derision, "Sing to us, O monks, your songs of praise!" And, armed with sticks and branches cut from trees, they brutally struck the brave martyrs. If any of them ceased from singing, either from fatigue or pain, the assaults upon him would be renewed with fresh vigor and viciousness.

Meanwhile, the Count of Lummen rode before them on a horse, inflated with his customary diabolical arrogance. In his hand he bore a heavy staff, and from time to time would strike his prisoners as if they were dogs or swine. How the spirit of hatred and brutality animated the citizens of Brielle is quite astonishing—it was as if they were infected with some virus of rabid madness or possessed by some demon which robbed them of their humanity and decency. For there was no restraint or measure to their mockery, brutality and cruelty.

Amongst the Franciscans, there was one—Jerome of Weert—who had made a pilgrimage to the Holy Land. There he had witnessed first-hand the nefarious and cruel customs and practices of the Turks, Greeks and Saracens; and had, in fact, been kidnapped and held captive by them for some time. But now he exclaimed, "Oh, where does this appalling barbarism which I now witness come from?! What race of people is there which is so alien to humanity and civilization to treat its captives in this way? For I have, in the past, fallen into the hands of the Turks, the Greeks and the Saracens. Yet even they would not degrade themselves by treating defenseless prisoners in this way!"

After they had been compelled to march through the streets in this manner, they eventually arrived at the city square. Whipping posts had been raised there, and again the friars and their companions were forced to process around them, singing litanies to the saints and hymns to the Virgin Mother of God. Of course, the Calvinists compelled them to sing these holy canticles as a means of mocking that which was sacred to their Catholic victims. Nevertheless, the friars themselves sang with the utmost sincerity. Though it was their persecutors who forced them to perform these acts of piety, they offered them to the glory of God and his holy Mother with reverence and love.

In truth, there is no power in the world which can prevent faithful Catholics from offering prayer, either with their voices, or at least in their hearts. Though the wicked persecutors demands that the friars sing were motivated by ill will and intended to be an insult and work of sacrilege, nevertheless the action which they demanded—namely, the offering of praise to God and veneration of the Blessed Virgin and the saints—was intrinsically good. Truly, we ourselves should never omit any act of piety on account of the fact that it may arouse scorn or derision in the minds of the wicked. For such things, however small, offer a living testimony to our faith. It behooves us not only to be ready to be mocked or treated with scorn for our religion, but indeed to die for it!

When the enforced procession of these heroic and faithful men had ended and they stood by the whipping posts, they were assaulted not only with derisions and insults but also with blows, kicks and spitting. And no consideration or pity was shown on account of the venerable age of some of them; for, in fact, one was in his sixties, another in his seventies and a third was in his nineties. And this abuse, both verbal and physical, was poured out by the entire crowd, comprising members of both sexes.

These men suffered their punishment of flogging, which was administered without measure or law. But before receiving this official punishment at the hands of the appointed officer, they had already been brutally abused by the ungodly mob. Truly, they had as many punishers as they had spectators!

What is this perplexing and inhuman cruelty to which heresy always gives birth? What is the origin of such inhumanity? For even the barbaric and primitive peoples display habitual respect and kindness to the elderly, nor do they permit any human being—even thieves, murderers and rebels—to be subjected to such revolting treatment.

But to continue with the account of the atrocities suffered by these men, they were now led away to a most loathsome prison, filled with filth and squalor. The dungeons to which they were taken were underground and constructed underneath the main prison building. All the excrement and sewage from the main prison was channeled into these subterranean cells, in such a way that their rank foulness and disgusting stench can hardly be imagined.

From this place of incarceration, in due course they were taken to the city hall, to appear before the Count of Lummen. They were not accused of any substantial crimes, but merely of being loyal to the Catholic Church—which, of course, they were quite ready to confess. An attempt was made to coerce them to betray their faith. Above all, they were promised that if they renounced their loyalty to the Roman Pontiff they should readily evade death. But they responded bravely that they would much rather die than commit such an act of apostasy and schism.

Various points of faith and theology were then discussed and disputed. But the responses of the friars were so clear, logical and well-founded that their Calvinist opponents soon dropped their vain and specious attempts at argument, and resorted to crude and violent threats— namely, that of the hangman's noose. The wretched Count himself spoke words of the most insane hatred, his reason and restraint all cast aside by the demonical arrogance and malice which possessed him.

Without going into detail, the result of this acrimonious farce which absurdly passed for a legitimate juridical process was that the friars and their associates were all sentenced to death by hanging. They were then returned to the tenebrous and tomb-like shadows of their squalid, subterranean dungeons.

*   *   *

That night, the haughty and barbaric Count of Lummen partook of particularly extravagant and depraved feasting. After pouring copious quantities of wine and spirits down his throat, he was bloated with liquor and hopelessly intoxicated. In his advanced state of drunkenness, a demonic fury took possession of him and his bestial hatred of the friars goaded him on to violence. So, at about eleven o'clock, he demanded that the sentence of death which had been passed against the prisoners should be carried out forthwith. Of course, the carrying out of a capital sentence at that time of night is something utterly bizarre and irregular, yet the inebriated Count insisted stubbornly.

His soldiers therefore took them from the cells where they were being held, and led them forth, accompanied by the clamor of arms and horses. It was then about the hour of midnight. Now, there still remained in the city of Brielle a former monastery of the Canons Regular of the Order of St. Augustine. The Calvinists had arrested these men and confiscated their property, which was at that time being used as a barn. Nooses were suspended from the rafters of this building, and from these the prisoners were hanged.

The treatment given to Jerome of Weert, who had made a pilgrimage to Jerusalem at one time, was particularly cruel. According to the common custom of people who have made this pilgrimage, Jerome had the form of a Jerusalem cross tattooed upon his chest and his right arm. The soldiers, when they saw this, seized the dagger and deeply carved the same form into the living flesh of the poor friar's face!

One of the Franciscans, just as he was about to be hanged, followed the example of Christ his Lord, exclaiming, "Father, forgive them, for they know not what they do!"

There was also a diocesan priest amongst those who were martyred, a Fr. Leonard van Veghel. He was a deeply learned and pious man. The torments and abuses he suffered during his time of captivity were so great that they may hardly be put into words. Then there was another member of the secular clergy—a gifted preacher and eminent theologian—who ascended the makeshift gallows to accept death without the slightest trace of trepidation or concern, freely offering his life for Christ and for the faith of the Roman Church.

The next to die was a younger diocesan priest, a youth of the highest devotion and distinction. Then followed another priest of the diocese of Gorkum. He was a man who was already in his seventies and who had cultivated the most perfect piety, innocence and chastity throughout his long life of ministry. Like his companions, he died with equanimity and calm patience. Along with these was executed a canon of the Order of St. Augustine, who had acted as chaplain to a convent of nuns of the same order. He, who was also elderly, did not fear the bitterness of shame of death in the least, but rather was animated by a passionate longing for the glorious palm of martyrdom. This he attained with heroic virtue and stainless courage.

Apart from these and the eleven Franciscan friars, there was also a Dominican who had been captured at Gorkum and shipped to Brielle with the friars and was martyred with them. There were also two Norbertine canons, who had been captured by forces from Geneva while at sea —for the Calvinists engaged in expeditions of piracy at that time. Finally, there was another member of the diocesan clergy, Fr. Andrew Wouters, the parish priest of Heinenoord near Dordrecht, who had been seized by heretic raiding parties

Even after all of these faithful servants of the Catholic Church had given up their lives as testament to their love for Christ, the cruelty and hatred of the schismatics was not satisfied. For they still hungered to perpetrate further acts of unspeakable depravity, and to desecrate the lifeless corpses of their innocent victims in the most revolting ways. They began by stripping off all their clothes. At once they severed the ears from all of them, and—it makes one shudder to think of it—hacked off other parts of the bodies. These the soldiers affixed to their helmets, as a ludicrous and obscene form of jest.

Next, in the manner of deranged butchers, they sliced up the bodies into pieces, opening their abdomens and removing their entrails. Now it should be noted that the body of Fr. Jerome of Weert was inordinately fat—for, to speak the truth without euphemism or polite blandishment, this unfortunate friar was, in fact, enormously obese. His murderers bound his deceased corpse to a rack and systematically carved him up with their daggers, removing copious quantities of adipose tissue in large, bloody slabs. They similarly removed the fatty portions from the bodies of the other martyrs, too.

These heinous deeds having been completed, the guards next made a grotesque procession through the city.

They carried aloft blubbery portions of Fr. Jerome's ample corpse and hunks of fat from the others as a kind of macabre trophy, their helmets still adorned with the severed body parts of their victims. Such is the perversity which can rise up in human beings, when infected with the Satanic venom of heresy and maddened with intoxicating liquors, that they considered all this to be a most merry caper!

After marching around the city in this way for some time, they eventually disposed of the slabs of human fat by selling them to people engaged in the perfume trade. And these callous purchasers of these disgusting goods used them in the manufacture of scents. For some time afterwards, it was possible to hear peddlers of perfumes in various city squares offering for sale scents which they openly claimed were manufactured from the remains of one friar or another.

The atrocities committed by all tyrants against the faithful are always to be deplored, such as those of the pagans of imperial Rome who threw Christians to lions and other beasts. Yet the cruelty of these former martyrdoms seems mild in comparison to the revolting obscenities of the schismatics of our own times, who seem to have entirely transgressed all the bounds of humanity. If we study the annals of the ancient Church and the martyrdoms of past ages, do we ever encounter such ghoulish abuses of the bodies of the dead? Do we ever find such demonic savagery and such insane hatred of Christ and his servants?

After the killing of these nineteen brave martyrs and the desecration of their bodies, what was left of their remains were suspended from gallows in the city. A great number of citizens—those whose minds were blinded by poison of Calvinist heresy—came to affix their eyes upon this "beautiful" spectacle, taking fiendish delight in the great number of priests and religious to have died in one place at one time. The nude and mutilated bodies of these saints hung helpless and stripped, exposed to the cruel and malicious gaze of the demonic mob.

Illustration XIII
The Franciscan Martyrs of Gorkum

The following events are depicted in Illustration XIII:

A (left side of the illustration): Fr. Nicolas Pieck, superior of the Franciscan friary at Gorkum, along with ten of friars of that order, as well as a number of other religious and diocesan, were forced to march in procession around the gallows, chanting the *Salve Regina.* All the while they were cruelly mocked and insulted by their persecutors. Finally, they were all hanged to death, some nineteen in altogether, on July 9, 1572.

B (middle right side of illustration): The bodies of those martyred in this atrocity were not allowed to rest in peace. On the contrary, the bodies were hung up like animal carcasses, and then were mutilated and desecrated. The fatty tissue and other parts were sold for use in commercial purposes.

C (left background): The same William de la Marck, the godless Count of Lummen, who had led the slaughter of the Franciscan friars of Gorkum, killed a certain priest in the Dutch city of Gouda, by nailing him to a cross. This was then suspended in the air from the gallows, for passers-by to see.

IV. The Martyrdom of Twelve Carthusian Monks at Roermond in Holland

I n the year of our Lord 1572, on the day following the feast of St. Mary Magdalene (that is, July 23), the Prince of Orange and his forces—or you could well call them the 'Army of Hell'—invaded the Dutch city of Roermond. Amidst the general devastation wrought by these ravenous aggressors, our own community of Carthusians at that location sustained the most dire damage and injustice. This was not only in the form of the confiscation and theft of the temporal possessions of the monastery, but also in injuries to, and even murder of, members of the Order. Several monks and lay brothers of the community were cruelly slaughtered at the hands of the pernicious heretics. Nevertheless, we confidently believe that God shall provide recompense for these deaths, by bestowing upon the victims all heavenly graces and the glorious crown of holy martyrdom.

In those days, the Carthusian monastery at Roermond was flourishing. It was well endowed both in respect to its material assets and in the sanctity and talents of the monks and brothers who comprised the community. This community consisted of fifteen professed monks, one visiting monk from the monastery at Koblenz, and eight lay brothers. We shall briefly describe the fate of each of these below.

Amongst these, the venerable Prior of the monastery, Fr. Joachim van Congerlo, holds primacy of place. He was seized in the tumult of the initial storming of the monastery, and then subjected to numerous tortures. Finally, he was released in return for payment of a large ransom, and fled to Cologne. Yet, due to the injuries and trauma he had sustained, he was to die very shortly afterwards. His mortal remains were buried in his city of refuge.

The second person in seniority was the deputy prior, a man by the name of Fr. Jan Voeren. He was captured and likewise subject to many afflictions and threats of death. But eventually he succeeded in escaping and took to flight. He lived on until 1579.

In third place was Fr. Wilhelm Willens, a senior monk of the community. He was captured and subject to severe beatings and abuses. But he managed to evade both death and the clutches of his captors and fled to the Carthusian monastery near Jülich in Germany. He lived there for precisely a year after his escape, and then passed away.

Fourth, Fr. Matthias of Cologne, a man of elderly years, was killed in his monastic cell, or the doorway of his cell.

Fifth, Fr. Erasmus of Utrecht was killed as he was walking towards the monastery church. He was a frail and aged man, and so supporting himself with a walking stick as he hobbled along the path towards the church. His assailants seized his staff from him. They then used his erstwhile instrument of support as a lethal weapon, stabbing him cleanly through the chest with it.

Sixth, Fr. Johannes of Utrecht was captured, but then released after payment of a ransom. He made his way to Cologne, suffering from a serious wound to his arm and lacerations to his head made with a two-edged sword.

Seventh, Fr. Vincent ab Herck, who served as sacristan for the monastery, was captured by the soldiers. These attacked him with ferocious beatings and cruel mockery. Then his torn, bruised and bleeding body was mercilessly dragged through the streets of the city. At the distant gates of the municipality he was killed, through a combination of sword wounds and musket shots. Certain good Catholics of the city took care to ensure that the mortal remains of this holy man were honorably buried.

Eighth was Fr. Jean of Liège. He was murdered while he was in choir, praying the Divine Office. The schismatics shot him with a burning lead bullet, which went straight through his head and shattered his skull to tiny fragments.

Ninth, Fr. Wilhelm Wellem, the procurator of the community, was also attacked while in prayer in the oratory. He was grievously wounded with a double-edged sword. After this, he was led out to the square in front of the monastery gates and there shot dead.

Tenth, Fr. Leonard of Liège managed to escape in a marvelous fashion, but not without wounds and scars from the many tortures he underwent.

In the eleventh place was Fr. Severus, a monk who was a guest from the Carthusian monastery near the German town of Koblenz. His assailants set upon him as he knelt in prayer before an altar of the Blessed Virgin Mary. They struck him with swords, and his blood spurted out so violently that stains from it were to be seen on the wall of the chapel at a height of some eighteen feet. His body was atrociously abused and defiled by the heretics. Indeed, the next day, remains of it were discovered in the kitchen. Mercifully perhaps, it is not clear precisely what horrendous things the schismatic butchers did to him there.[2] Nor is it clear if he was killed in the chapel and afterwards taken to the kitchen, or if he was dragged from the chapel still alive to the kitchen, and there surrendered his spirit to God.

Next, in the twelfth place, was Fr. John Lewis, whom the schismatics seized whilst he was praying the Divine Office in the monastery oratory. They brutally broke both of his shoulders. Then, while he writhed in agony, they drove an iron spike through his still beating heart.

Thirteenth was Fr. Jan Asz. After being beaten and wounded, a certain soldier (who still retained a fragment of humanity in his soul) kindly spared the holy man's life from the brutal assaults of the others. In return for a ransom, he was set free and lived on to survive until 1579.

---

[2] The suggestion here seems to be that the heretics may have indulged in acts of cannibalism.

Fourteenth was Nicolaus Ganglet, a deacon. By assuming a clever disguise, he managed to escape from his captors. Nevertheless, he carried with him a multitude of severe wounds from the tortures he had received.

Fifteenth was Heinrich Wellen, also a deacon. He was the first one of the professed monks to be martyred, being savagely pierced through with a stake before the high altar.

Sixteenth was Johannes Gressenich, another deacon, whose death was particularly horrible. He was stabbed through the back, until the blade penetrated into the depths of his lungs. Yet, though he was in a wretched state and close to death, he managed to escape and drag himself to the town of Maaseick. There a certain Catholic surgeon diligently attended to him, but his patient soon died as a result of his injuries. His body was reverently interred at the monastery of the Order of the Cross-bearers at Maaseick.

These are all the solemnly professed Carthusian monks who were at Roermond—both priests and deacons—of whom nine were martyred. Seven received serious wounds and injuries as a result of tortures, but survived with their lives, in most cases only after the payment of considerable ransoms.

We shall now turn our attention to the lay brothers and oblates amongst the community. Of these, three were killed for their faith, who are named below. Thus the holy number of twelve martyrs referred to in the title of this chapter was fulfilled.

Brother Stephen, who was gatekeeper to the monastery, was the first to encounter the soldiers of the heretics as the sought ingress into the monastic cloister. Indeed, it was he who opened the gates for them. For this act of courtesy and hospitality, he was horribly beaten to death by the soldiers almost immediately.

Brother Albert was the cook for the community. At that time, he was ill and lay in his bed. With neither mercy nor compassion, the marauders forcibly dragged him out, and killed the sick man in the doorway of his cell.

Finally, Brother Johannes Sittard was the baker of the monastery. On becoming aware of the invading heretics, he concealed himself under a pile of firewood. But—alas!—they soon discovered the hapless brother in his place of hiding, and promptly dispatched him to his Creator.

Illustration XIV
The Carthusian Martyrs at Roermond

The following events are depicted in Illustration XIV:

A (foreground of illustration): The monks of the Carthusian monastery at Roermond were killed, injured or brutally persecuted by Calvinist heretics This included slaughtering four of them as they were devoutly praying the Divine Office.

B (middle right side of illustration): Fr. Severus, a monk from Germany who was visiting the monastery at Roermond as a guest, was sent to his death by a blow of the sword as he knelt in fervent prayer before an altar dedicated to the Blessed Virgin. So violent was the blow with which he was struck that his blood splattered high upon the walls of the chapel.

V. Other Atrocities
Committed by the Calvinists
in Holland and Flanders

There is a certain ancient and picturesque town in northern Holland, called Alkmaar. Now this town, like many others in Holland, was invaded and captured by the forces of the Calvinist heretics. There was a religious house of Franciscan friars there. This house was seized, and the friars were all arrested and sent to the city Enschede. After being subject to various forms of torture, the friars were eventually hanged, and so became martyrs for their faith.

Amongst these Franciscans was one particular lay brother called Engelbert, who was a simple and devout man. His captors came to learn that he had been entrusted with the custody of the gold and silver of his religious house, and so they singled him out, demanding that he procure for them the treasures for which he was responsible. When he refused to do this, the wicked and greedy captors subjected him to an astounding range of cruel tortures. He was first stretched out on a rack, and then tied up by his hands and feet and hung aloft. While thus suspended, flaming torches were applied to him, scorching various parts of his body.

A certain obscene and unspeakable brew had been concocted by the soldiers, which was poured down the unfortunate friar's throat. Then his savage persecutors doused him with boiling water and scalded him all over, before scourging him mercilessly with whips. For several months, they tortured him incessantly in this manner. But, like St. Laurence, he adamantly refused to betray the treasures of the holy Church even when subject to the extremity of pain and remained unwavering in his fidelity. Finally, he was dispatched to the region of Randsdorp, within sight of the city of Amsterdam. There he was hanged to death, and thus attained the glorious crown of martyrdom.

Again in Holland, a certain man, Johannes Hieronymus by name, was arrested together with various other Catholics and taken to the Hague. There they were subjected to the most ruthless beatings, no less than eight times. The soldiers of the heretics tortured them with fearsome cruelty. As a final act of savagery, they laid the men on their backs, stripped naked, and then placed inverted basins, filled with furious rats, on their abdomens. This was done in such a manner that the rodents were trapped within the basins on the men's stomachs. The schismatic villains then lit a fire above the basins. The rats, maddened by the heat of the fire and their close captivity, began to gnaw desperately into the innards of the victims in an effort to escape, eventually penetrating deeply into the cavities of their viscera.

In Flanders not far from the city of Ypres, many priests were captured. The cruel heretics then buried them alive in the earth, with only their heads protruding from the ground. Then, as a kind of game, they stood a certain distance away from the buried men and rolled spheres of stone or metal at them, using their exposed heads as targets!

The city of Oudenaarde was similarly captured and occupied by heretics from Geneva. As in other places, they hunted down all Catholic priests and arrested them. These were subject to their customary heinous abuse— namely, beatings, false and slanderous accusations and insults and humiliations of all kinds. Monasteries, churches and religious houses were raided and robbed, and everything of value which could be extracted was taken. In the principal church of that town, some thirty-six valuable chalices fell prey to the sacrilegious theft of the schismatics. There were various other acts of pillage and plunder which I shall pass over in silence, for they are too many to be enumerated.

The heretics also invaded one particular religious house of Franciscan friars in the same city of Oudenaarde. And they left not a single lock or wall or window unbroken. The tombs of the dead and sacred altars alike were desecrated, and church bells were stolen. They insulted the friars maliciously, calling them wolves, morons and lunatics. And not only this, but they seized upon them and beat them, and threatened them by holding swords and rifles to their chests and throats.

Among this community of friars there was a holy and learned man of the most distinguished virtue called Johannes Mahusius. He had been chosen as Bishop of the Dutch city of Deventer—but due to his advanced age and physical infirmity, he had never been able to take up residence in that diocese. Despite the venerable age and illustrious status of this man, they insulted him with cruel jokes and inane mockery. They pinched and slapped him viciously, then dragged him out of his bed where he lay on account of his illness. Hurling him to the floor, they kicked and shoved him around violently, all the while howling with diabolical laughter.

We will not neglect to mention the horrible ordeal by which the superior of the community of Franciscans at Zutphen was put to death. His entrails were cut out, and he was hanged along with six other friars. Such horrors are a testimony both to the depravity of the enemies of the Church, and of the fidelity and courage of its loyal sons.

Many other unspeakable crimes are able to be related concerning religious of other orders. In some places, they were brutally beheaded. There were also many members of the diocesan clergy and even Catholic lay people who were victims of the sacrilegious hands of these wicked and bloodthirsty tyrants.

Illustration XV

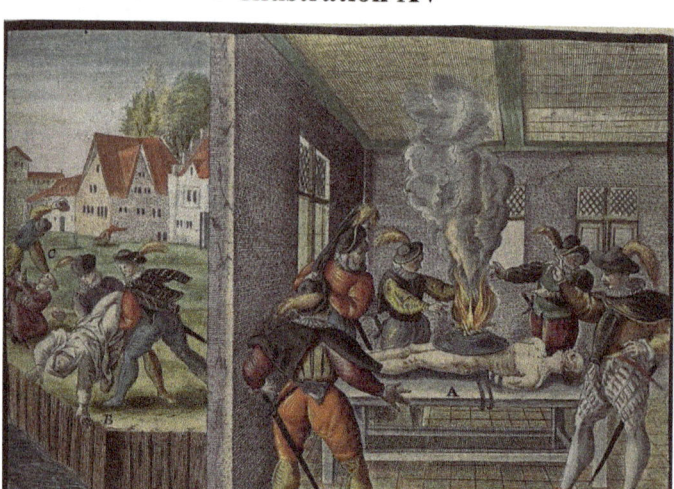

The following events are depicted in Illustration XV:

A (right side of illustration): A certain man, Johannes Hieronymus by name, was arrested together with various other Catholics and taken to the Hague. After inflicting severe beating, they laid the men on their backs, stripped naked, and then placed inverted basins, filled with furious rats, on their abdomens. This was done in such a manner that the rodents were trapped within the basins on the men's stomachs. The schismatic villains then lit a fire above the basins. The rats, maddened by the heat of the fire and their close captivity, began to gnaw desperately into the innards of the victims in an effort to escape, eventually penetrating deeply into the cavities of their viscera. This, of course, caused unimaginable pain.

B (left side foreground): A certain nun, Sr. Ursula Talisia, was captured by heretics in the Dutch city of Harlem. Many of her sisters in religion were hanged or strangled, but she was told that she could escape death if she agreed to marry one of the Calvinist soldiers, who admired her appearance. She refused, however, and so was drowned in the waters of a local canal.

C (left midground): The married sister of the abovementioned Sr. Ursula mourned her sibling's cruel and unjust death with heartfelt and sincere sorrow. As she refused to stop her crying at her sister's cruel death, one of the heretics struck her on the head with a large stone with such force that her skull was cracked upon, and her brain splattered all over her face.

VI. The Cruelties of the Protestants in England under the Reign of Queen Elizabeth I

Illustration XVI

The following events are depicted in the Illustration XVI:

A (lower right side of illustration): Catholic priests were compelled to celebrate the Mass in secret locations during the tyrannical reign of Elizabeth I. These Masses were often attended by many of those who secretly remained faithful to the true Church. Whenever these gatherings were detected, all involved would be marched through the town squares and then cast into prison.

B (lower left side): The houses and estates of those who remained true to the Catholic faith were invaded, raided, then unlawfully occupied by the heretics. The rightful owners were then led off into wretched captivity.

C (right midground): Priests and bishops who were loyal to the Catholic Church were forced to wear their sacred vestments and were then led through the town squares mounted on horses. While this was happening, they were subjected to disrespectful and blasphemous mockeries for their persecutors.

D: (slightly to the right in the background of the illustration): Captured Catholics were led, two by two, into prisons. After an initial period of incarceration, they would then be taken to even more wretched places of confinement.

Illustration XVII

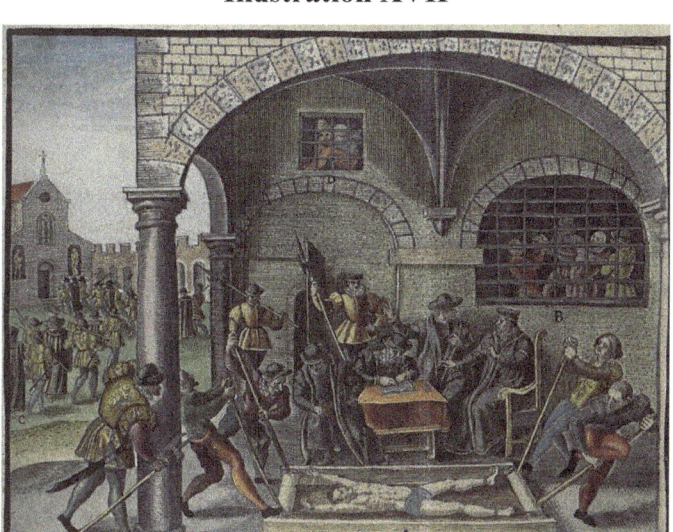

The following events are depicted in Illustration XVII:

A (center foreground): Priests, and especially Jesuits, were cruelly tortured in order to compel them to betray their religious confreres. Often there were incarcerated in the dreaded Tower of London. The illustration shows one captured priest suffering gravely on the rack, a common device of torture used to stretch the body of the victim in an exceedingly painful manner.

B (center midground): Iron nails and sharp pieces of metal were often forced under the fingernails of priests, as a further method of torture.

C (left midground): Faithful Catholic who were captured were compelled by force to listen to sermons delivered by heretical preachers.

D: (upper center): One of the most notorious and dreaded places of confinement in England was known as *Little Ease.* It was a cell in the Tower of London so small that it was impossible for any prisoner being held therein to stand, or sit, or lie down.

Illustration XVIII
The Execution of Mary, Queen of Scots

Mary, the most serene Queen of Scotland and legitimate heir to the crown of England, was the daughter of King James V and the mother of James VI of Scotland. She was born to the noble house of Guise on her mother's side, and (unlike Elizabeth, her half-sister) she was the daughter of Henry VIII of a *legitimate* marriage, and therefore the true heir of the English crown. Queen Mary was severely afflicted by the evil of heretics in her own Kingdom of Scotland. This is a nation which, alas, does not hesitate to persecute its legitimate rulers, and which is now infected with schismatic pride and therefore despoiled of all its humanity!

In England, at the urging and initiative of Queen Elizabeth, she entered into a treaty of peace and perpetual friendship. But the first fruit of heresy is always treachery, and so Elizabeth promptly betrayed this treaty, spurning the oaths and pledges with which it had been sealed. Thus is was that Mary was seized and cast into prison at the behest of her wicked half-sister, Elizabeth.

Mary was held in captivity for almost twenty years, frequently being moved from one place of incarceration to another. Nevertheless, despite all that she suffered, she remained unwaveringly faithful to Our Lord Jesus Christ and His holy Catholic Church.

In contempt of all justice, law and honor, Mary was executed in Fotheringhay Castle, on February 8, 1587. She was killed with a cruel blow from an axe, which severed her head from her body.

This wonderful queen was endowed by Heaven with great gifts of both body and soul. There is no person who is of such inhumanity that, if they saw her with their own eyes, would not greatly admire her, and be moved to the deepest compassion and pity for her undeserved plight. But Elizabeth, the cruel parricide,[3] could not even bear the sight of her. Indeed, Elizabeth was fearful that when the excellence, constancy and courage of Mary where seen by others, her own mistreatment of Mary would not be tolerated.

The faith and constancy of this martyr and Queen have rendered her beloved and revered, both in Heaven and on earth. Her history is described in more detail in other sources. Nevertheless, we pray that almighty God will deign—through the sword of some faithful Christian king—to obtain justice against the barbaric tyrant, Elizabeth, for her wicked injuries to His Holy Name and her cruel and heartless crimes committed against His holy Catholic Church.[4]

---

[3] A murderer of a sibling or close relative.
[4] When this work was originally published (1578), Elizabeth I was still alive.